Cambridge **Discovery Education**™

▶ **INTERACTIVE READERS**

Series editor: Bob Hastings

DEEP BLUE
DISCOVERING THE SEA

B1+

Caroline Shackleton and Nathan Paul Turner

 CAMBRIDGE UNIVERSITY PRESS

 ⊕DISCOVERY EDUCATION™

CAMBRIDGE
UNIVERSITY PRESS

University Printing House, Cambridge CB2 8BS, United Kingdom

One Liberty Plaza, 20th Floor, New York, NY 10006, USA

477 Williamstown Road, Port Melbourne, VIC 3207, Australia

314–321, 3rd Floor, Plot 3, Splendor Forum, Jasola District Centre, New Delhi – 110025, India

79 Anson Road, #06–04/06, Singapore 079906

Cambridge University Press is part of the University of Cambridge.

It furthers the University's mission by disseminating knowledge in the pursuit of education, learning and research at the highest international levels of excellence.

www.cambridge.org
Information on this title: www.cambridge.org/9781107697058

First published 2014

20 19 18 17 16 15 14 13 12 11 10 9 8

Printed in Dubai by Oriental Press

A catalogue record for this publication is available from the British Library.

Library of Congress Cataloguing in Publication data
Shackleton, Caroline.
 Deep blue : discovering the sea / Caroline Shackleton and Nathan Paul Turner.
    pages cm. -- (Cambridge discovery interactive readers)
  ISBN 978-1-107-69705-8 (pbk. : alk. paper)
  1. Ocean--Juvenile literature. 2. English language--Textbooks for foreign speakers.
  3. Readers (Elementary) I. Title.

GC21.5.S49 2013
551.46--dc23

                                        2013024753

ISBN 978-1-107-69705-8

Additional resources for this publication at www.cambridge.org

Layout services, art direction, book design, and photo research: Q2ABillSMITH GROUP
Editorial services: Hyphen S.A.
Audio production: CityVox, New York
Video production: Q2ABillSMITH GROUP

Contents

Before You Read: Get Ready!

The sea covers 71 percent of our planet, but what exactly is under all that water?

Look at the pictures. Then complete the sentences below with the correct words.

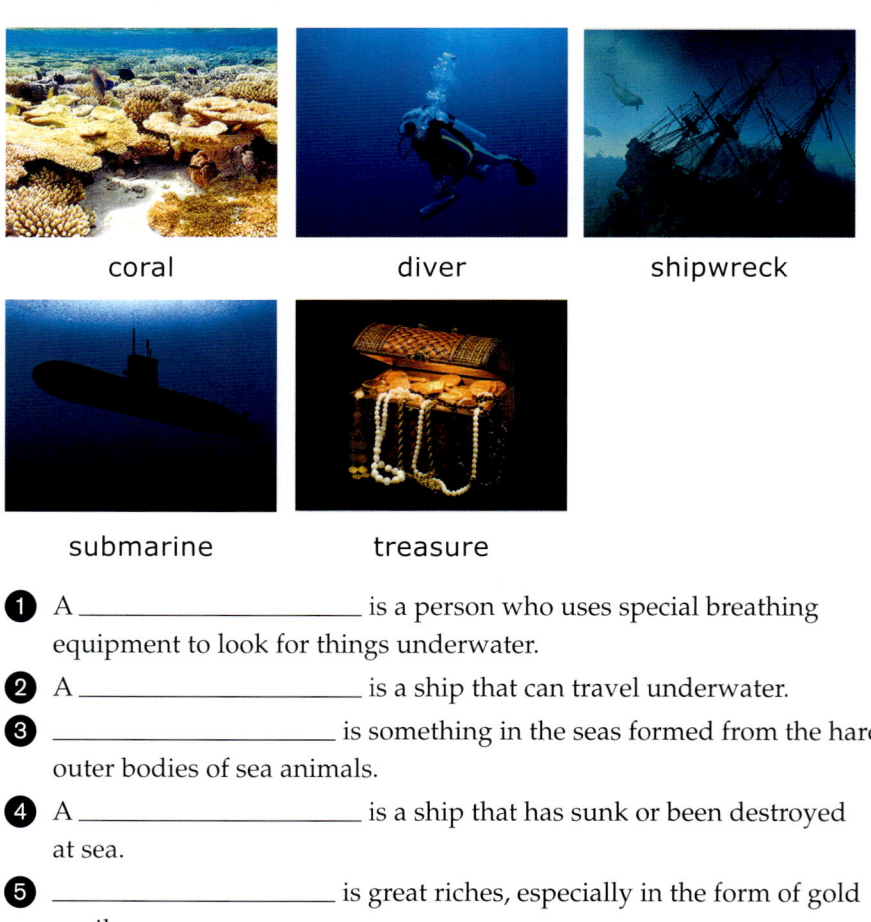

coral   diver   shipwreck

submarine   treasure

❶ A _____ is a person who uses special breathing equipment to look for things underwater.

❷ A _____ is a ship that can travel underwater.

❸ _____ is something in the seas formed from the hard outer bodies of sea animals.

❹ A _____ is a ship that has sunk or been destroyed at sea.

❺ _____ is great riches, especially in the form of gold or silver.

Read the paragraph. Then complete the definitions below with the correct highlighted words.

On April 28, 1947, six men set off from Peru on a voyage of discovery. They wanted to try to cross the Pacific Ocean in a small raft made from a very light wood, called balsa. This raft floated on the surface of the water. The name of the boat was the *Kon-Tiki*. The leader, a Norwegian named Thor Heyerdahl, wanted to prove that it had been possible for people from South America to navigate as far as the islands of Polynesia. After 101 days at sea, the group arrived safely on a Polynesian island. The voyage had not been easy. Heyerdahl said there were times when he was afraid for his life. He later wrote a book about his journey, *The Kon-Tiki Expedition*.

1 _____ : a flat boat made of pieces of wood tied together

2 _____ : a long trip, especially by ship

3 _____ : the top part of something

4 _____ : move a ship or other vehicle across an area of water or land

CHAPTER 1

Humans and the Sea

KAIKEA LOOKED UP AT THE STARS, FOLLOWING THE PATH THAT HE KNEW WOULD KEEP THE CANOE ON COURSE. . . .

He was still only a young boy, but he knew all the traveling songs and stories. His father had sung them to him since before he could remember. He looked down at his father who was finally resting. How tired he must be! The big storm had thrown the boats in so many directions, and his father had spent three days without sleep before finding the other families. He was a great sailor.

They had little food or water left, but they had seen birds, so land must be near. They would be safe now, as long as the weather stayed calm. Kaikea sang his own name quietly to himself as he watched the stars. It made him feel safer. "Kaikea . . . Clear sea, clear sea . . ."

Scientists believe that people first started leaving Africa about 100,000 years ago, moving into parts of Europe and Asia, Australia, and the Americas. To do this, they made boats strong enough to cross rivers, lakes, and seas.

Australian Aborigines crossed the sea from Asia as early as 50,000 years ago. They probably used simple rafts made from whole trees tied together.

It seems that a lot of early exploration[1] was done by small family groups who **navigated** their rafts slowly along the coasts of Europe and Asia. This was for a very simple reason; it was very difficult and dangerous for these early travelers to move through the thick forests that covered most of the land. Most people lived and worked along the rivers and coasts, which allowed them to eat, drink, and travel more easily.

....
[1] **exploration:** going to and learning about a completely new place

A traditional canoe

Many cultures have such a close relationship with the sea that it becomes part of their social identity. Often, these are island communities² that depend on boats to travel and catch food.

Pacific South Sea island cultures, such as the Polynesians and the New Zealand Maoris, are famous for being able to navigate thousands of kilometers in their traditional canoes without maps. Between about 3000 and 1000 BCE, these people emigrated³ from southeast Asia across the Pacific Ocean, arriving in New Zealand, Samoa, and as far away as Hawaii.

Their knowledge of the islands, seas, winds, and stars were passed down in songs that allowed them to remember even the smallest details.

....

²**community:** all the people who live in a particular area
³**emigrate:** leave your own country or area to live in another place

For thousands of years, people have used the sea for **trade**. The earliest picture of a boat with a sail was painted on an Egyptian vase about 5000 BCE.

By the 1st century CE, Roman and Greek sailors were traveling across the Mediterranean Sea, through the Arabian Gulf, and across to India. Gold Roman coins have been found in Southern India. Some Roman writers even complained about how much Roman gold was being spent on Indian silk[4] and spices![5]

And yet, the sea has always been something to fear. Its power and size has led to many stories about huge **creatures** called sea monsters. Even today, many people continue to search for signs of sea monsters, such as Scotland's famous Loch Ness Monster!

But this **fascination** with monsters might not be as crazy as it seems. As we are going to see, the world's seas hold many strange and terrifying creatures!

[4]**silk:** a smooth, shiny cloth
[5]**spices:** made from plants, they make foods taste special

Sailors told exciting stories about sea monsters.

?

UNDERSTAND

Why did the first explorers travel by sea? What did sea travel allow people to do?

A squid

CHAPTER 2

At the Bottom of the Sea

SOMETIMES TRUTH IS STRANGER THAN FICTION.

In 2007, fishermen from New Zealand made a strange and frightening catch off the coast of Antarctica. Instead of the fish they were hoping for, they caught a 13-meter-long squid, the biggest ever found! It weighed 495 kilograms and its eyes were 15 centimeters across! Its mouth, however, was a lot smaller than those of other squids that have been found. So, although it is the biggest squid ever caught, this squid could probably have grown even bigger!

Sailors used to tell stories of a monster as big as a small island that came from under the sea and swallowed[6] even the biggest ships whole. This monster of **legends**, known as the Kraken, may have been based upon sailor's experiences with giant squid like the one found by the fishermen from New Zealand.

....

[6]**swallow:** move food or drink from your mouth into your stomach

A Kraken was probably really a giant squid.

The Kraken is not the only horrible creature that sailors used to create stories about. In many cultures around the world there are all sorts of stories about strange sea monsters.

The Ancient Greeks told stories about a terrible monster called Scylla. Once a beautiful young girl, a jealous witch turned her into an enormous six-headed sea snake. Scylla waited for passing ships and jumped out from her cave, eating six men at a time with her monstrous mouths.

It is easy to understand why sailors created stories of incredible monsters lying in the depths of the sea. Animals that now seem normal to us seemed incredibly scary to people navigating the seas in small, easily wrecked, wooden boats.

? ANALYZE

Why did sailors in the past think there were monsters in the sea?

A frilled shark

Nowadays, we know a lot more about what lies below the surface of the waves. Thanks to new technology such as submarines, biologists in the 20th century were able to explore much more of the oceans and discover and record the existence of many amazing creatures. Some of them are at least as strange and terrifying as the monsters of legends.

One example is the snake-like frilled shark, which scientists think may have inspired[7] stories of sea monsters. Another is the strange 350-million-year-old coelacanth. Long believed extinct, or no longer living, this fish was re-discovered in 1938 in a South African fish market! When he saw it, one biologist said he was as surprised as if a dinosaur had walked down the street!

[7]**inspire:** give someone an idea

Video Quest

The Great Barrier Reef

Watch the video about the Great Barrier Reef. When did the coral start growing? How many types of fish are there?

A coelacanth

The discovery of the coelacanth proves that sea creatures can remain hidden from science and shows that we still have a lot to learn about the waters around us. The sea's mysteries and the possibilities of hidden monsters continue to fascinate the human imagination.

In May 2012, for example, a video of a strange sea creature was posted on the Internet. It seemed to be like no animal ever seen before and was given the name "Cascade Creature." Some people suggested that it was an alien from another planet or a monster from the depths of the sea. Others said it was just a plastic bag.

Finally, biologists cleared up the mystery. The strange creature was a type of jellyfish called *Deepstaria enigmatica*. Truth is definitely sometimes stranger than fiction.

CHAPTER 3

Conquered by the Sea

COLD, DEEP, DEADLY . . . THE SEA OFTEN TURNS AGAINST THOSE WHO LOVE HER.

In May 2007, a marine archaeological[8] team called Odyssey Marine found the wreck of the Spanish sailing ship *Nuestra Señora de Las Mercedes* off the south coast of Portugal.

In 1804, the *Mercedes* was returning from Peru carrying more than 15,000 kilograms of silver and gold. It was attacked by British ships and sunk.

The divers from Odyssey Marine brought up about 595,000 silver and gold coins, worth more than $500 million today! However, almost immediately an argument began over who owned the coins. Odyssey Marine argued that the **treasure** was private, and so it was theirs. The Spanish government argued that the ship belonged to Spain.

Finally, the courts[9] returned the treasure to Spain, where it was put in museums. The divers who found the treasure didn't get a single coin!

[8] **marine archaeology:** the study of ancient cultures through things found in the sea

[9] **court:** the place where arguments about the law happen

Scientists from the United Nations believe there are probably over three million **shipwrecks** lying on the seafloor. Like the *Mercedes*, ships can sink from attacks at sea, but they can sink for many other reasons, too: fire, hitting other ships or rocks, storms.

It is difficult to find older shipwrecks because these ships were made of wood, which is destroyed very quickly in salty seawater. Unless the ship is preserved[10] in sand, mostly all that remains of a wrecked ship are the parts made of metal. Of course, this is often what interests divers, because they are looking for valuable objects like coins and jewelry.

The oldest intact shipwreck ever found is believed to be from the 14th century CE. Scientists are hoping it might be one of the treasure ships of the Danish king Valdemar IV, which sank near Denmark while returning home after fighting in a war. The ship was supposedly full of gold and silver treasure, but so far it has not been found.

[10] **preserve:** protect something from being damaged or destroyed

As well as holding fabulous treasure, shipwrecks can tell us many things about everyday life in the historical times and places they come from. Many of the things we know about ancient civilizations, such as Greece and Rome, are thanks to objects that have been perfectly preserved at the bottom of the sea.

The many shipwrecks found in the Mediterranean contained wine, coins, tools,[11] and even medicines. A 2000-year-old ship found off the coast of Tuscany, in Italy, held glass bottles containing different medical pills made from plants and animals. By recognizing the plants in the pills, scientists were able to understand more about medicines of that time.

Sometimes, divers can even use what they find! Recently, more than a hundred bottles of 200-year-old French champagne were found in a wreck near Sweden. It was the oldest drinkable champagne in the world! In 2011 two of the bottles were sold together for the incredible price of $78,400!

Two of the most important shipwrecks are the Swedish warship *Vasa* and the English warship *Mary Rose*.

[11] **tool:** something you use with your hands to make or repair something

The badly designed *Vasa* sank in 1628 on its very first **voyage** when it hit a light wind! It was brought to the surface in 1961 and can be seen at the Vasa Museum in Stockholm. The ship held over 26,000 objects, including clothes, coins, and sculptures, and even a typical Swedish board game, called Tables.

The *Mary Rose*, the most important English warship of its time, was sunk in a battle against the French in 1545. In 1982, a team of scientists successfully floated the ship to the surface. Among the objects found on it were woodworking tools, musical instruments, and weapons.[12] These amazing discoveries have helped give scientists a new understanding of 16th-century technology.

[12] **weapon:** any object used in fighting or war, such as a gun or a bomb

Video Quest

Virtual Sea Experience: Part 1

Watch this video to learn about a virtual sea experience. What will be possible if the experiment works?

CHAPTER 4

Conquering the Sea

AS WE LEARN MORE ABOUT THE SEA, WE ALSO UNDERSTAND MORE ABOUT ITS VALUE TO US.

In 2007, six Italian scuba divers spent fourteen days living 15 meters under the sea.

The team lived on an underwater shelf on the Italian coast with special separate sleeping chambers,[13] which were tied to the rock. They could only take off their scuba equipment and breathe normally inside the chambers. The rest of the time they had to wear their masks and **tanks** in order to breathe.

Although they couldn't talk to each other, the team had activities and games to keep them busy, including a special underwater table for playing pool!

[13] **chamber:** a room or space used for a particular purpose

tank

mask

Doctors kept a continuous watch on the team to check that they were healthy. Amazingly, when they returned to the surface, they were found to be in perfect shape. This was the first test in the group's experiment to see if humans can live and work underwater.

Humans have always wanted to be part of the sea. There is a cave in Egypt called The Cave of Swimmers. On the walls are paintings that are about 10,000 years old. They show people swimming and diving. They are the earliest pictures of people swimming that have ever been found.

Seafood **shells** have also been discovered in places where many stone-age peoples lived. This suggests that people have dived in the sea for food since the earliest days of human society.

But swimmers have dived in the sea for more than food and shells. In many parts of the world, people have dived to find treasure from shipwrecks. And since ancient times, divers have gone to the bottom of the sea to find pearls.

A pearl

Traditional Polynesian cultures are famous for their pearl divers. These people can dive down more than 35 meters and hold their breath for more than two minutes. Traditional diving without using any equipment is known today as "free diving."

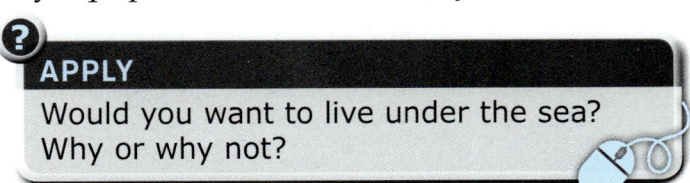

APPLY

Would you want to live under the sea?
Why or why not?

A diving bell

Humans began to make machines to dive longer and deeper thousands of years ago. The diving bell, which uses outside water pressure[14] to keep air inside it, was mentioned by Aristotle in the 4th century BCE. Alexander the Great supposedly used one to explore the Mediterranean seabed in the 3rd century BCE. Later, a similar bell was used to rescue objects from the Swedish warship *Vasa* in 1664.

In 1690, Dutchman Cornelius van Drebbel invented the first moving undersea submarine. His underwater boat moved under the River Thames in London for three hours.

The first military submarine was the *Turtle*, used by the Americans in their War of Independence in the late 18th century. It could only travel slowly because it used a hand-turned motor to move through the water.

[14] **pressure:** the strength of one thing pushing against another thing

Well before van Drebbel, in the 15th century, Leonardo da Vinci designed submarines and what look like suits that allowed divers to breathe underwater. Unfortunately, however, no explanations of these designs have ever been found.

One of the first diving suits we know about was made in 1715 by Chevalier de Beauve. It had a metal helmet[15] that received air through pipes. This became the model for many diving suits through the 18th and 19th centuries. These suits had heavy weights that held divers down and allowed them to walk along the bottom of the sea.

Diving suits were the most popular and useful form of diving until the invention in 1945 of the Aqua-Lung by the French engineer Emile Gagnan and the French underwater explorer Jacques Cousteau. The Aqua-Lung was a tank of air with a mask that allowed divers complete freedom of movement. Divers were free to explore the seas as they never had before.

[15]**helmet:** a hard hat that covers and protects the whole head

One of the scariest and most incredible things about the sea is how deep it is. The deepest point known is called Challenger Deep, near the Philippines. There, the sea is 10,994 kilometers deep. That's more than 10 times the height of Mount Everest, the world's highest mountain!

The record for the deepest dive in a scuba suit is presently 330 meters. To go deeper, humans need the protection of machines. One of the first deep-sea submarines, the Bathysphere, was built by the American engineer Otis Barton in 1930. Barton was lowered into the sea on a cable[16] to 900 meters under the surface.

Now, with better technology, people are going even deeper. In 2012, the movie director James Cameron took a specially designed deep-sea submarine, *Deepsea Challenger*, to the bottom of Challenger Deep, spending three hours exploring the deepest place on Earth!

[16] **cable:** thick strong rope or wire

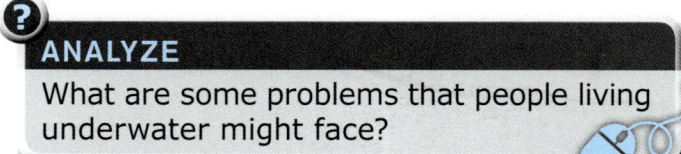

ANALYZE

What are some problems that people living underwater might face?

The longest time that anyone has lived underwater is 69 days. That record was set by Rick Presley from the United States who ate, worked, and slept in a specially built tank under a lake. By studying underwater living in experiments like this one, some scientists hope we may one day be able to build underwater cities.

Humans living and working permanently under the sea? It may sound like science fiction, but already one team of divers has planned the first human underwater colony.[17]

The colony, Atlantica I, is scheduled to begin in 2013 with a 90-day underwater stay in specially made living spaces called Leviathan Habitats. The team hopes that this will lead to a more permanent colony in the near future.

[17] **colony:** a group of people who live together

CHAPTER 5

What Do You Think?

SHOULD WE REALLY BE LOOKING TO THE SEA FOR OUR FUTURE?

The sea has played a huge part in human history. Now, people like Dennis Chamberland, the leader of the Atlantica team, believe that our future is tied to living in and exploring the depths of the seas and oceans.

Here are some different opinions about our future relationship with the sea. Which one(s) do you agree with and why?

1. With human populations growing bigger and bigger, our societies can only survive[18] by learning to live under the sea.

2. We should spend more money on protecting the environment we live in now rather than looking for new places to live under the sea.

3. Space exploration is a waste of money. We shouldn't go into space. We should explore the seas instead.

4. People were born to live on dry land, and the idea of living and working underwater is too scary and unnatural.

If people do start to live underwater, what do you think life will be like? What sort of jobs would people have? How might our bodies change because of living underwater? How might our personalities change?

[18]**survive:** continue to live or to exist, especially after a dangerous event

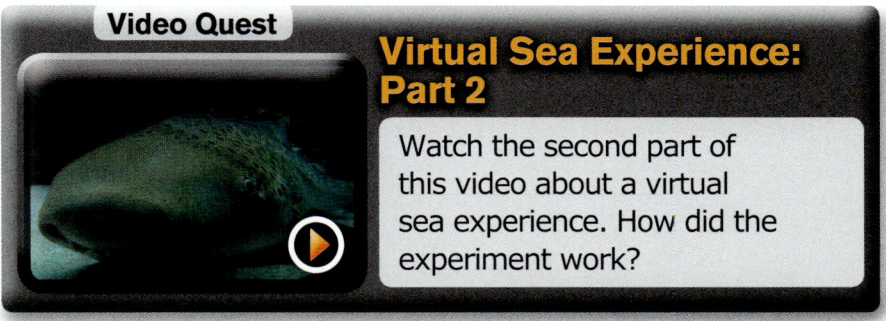

Video Quest

Virtual Sea Experience: Part 2

Watch the second part of this video about a virtual sea experience. How did the experiment work?

After You Read

Correctly complete each sentence by choosing Ⓐ, Ⓑ, Ⓒ, or Ⓓ.

❶ The New Zealand Maoris found their way on the sea using _____.

   Ⓐ detailed maps of the area
   Ⓑ boats that were made for rivers
   Ⓒ detailed plans of the islands
   Ⓓ information from their parents

❷ Some Roman writers complained about people _____.

   Ⓐ buying things from India
   Ⓑ selling Roman goods
   Ⓒ sailing on the sea
   Ⓓ spending time in India

❸ People said that the Kraken monster _____.

   Ⓐ had many heads
   Ⓑ lived in a cave
   Ⓒ ate ships whole
   Ⓓ was half human

❹ One country got back its treasure after _____.

   Ⓐ fighting a battle in the courts
   Ⓑ paying for an expensive exploration
   Ⓒ attacking and sinking a ship
   Ⓓ rescuing a ship from a storm

❺ The ship *Vasa* sank because _____.

   Ⓐ there was a storm
   Ⓑ there was a battle
   Ⓒ it wasn't well made
   Ⓓ it was carrying too much

6 During an experiment about living underwater, the people _____.

 Ⓐ swam all the time
 Ⓑ wore masks all the time
 Ⓒ didn't speak to each other
 Ⓓ didn't sleep very well

7 Early diving suits _____.

 Ⓐ were based on designs for submarines
 Ⓑ were based on da Vinci's designs
 Ⓒ included heavy weights
 Ⓓ included hand-turned motors

8 The person who has spent the longest time underwater lived _____.

 Ⓐ under the sea in a tank
 Ⓑ underwater for 69 days
 Ⓒ as part of a colony
 Ⓓ in a tank for 90 days

True or False?

Circle T (true) or F (false) for each statement.

1	Early travelers found it difficult to travel overland.	T	F
2	The biggest squid ever found was probably not the biggest that exists.	T	F
3	The Kraken was studied by scientists.	T	F
4	The Cascade Creature was really a type of jellyfish.	T	F
5	Portugal won a court battle over gold found on a shipwreck.	T	F
6	We can find out information about the past from shipwrecks.	T	F
7	Someone paid a lot of money for medicines found on a shipwreck.	T	F
8	Some underwater divers don't use special equipment.	T	F
9	Aristotle wrote about early diving equipment.	T	F
10	The *Turtle* was the first submarine.	T	F

Answer Key

Before You Read, page 4
1 diver **2** submarine **3** Coral **4** shipwreck **5** Treasure

Before You Read, page 5
1 raft **2** voyage **3** surface **4** navigate

Understand, page 9
They couldn't travel over the land because of the forests.
Sea travel allowed them to live and work more easily.

Analyze, page 11
They were not familiar with the animals that lived in the
sea, and the animals seemed strange and scary to them.

Video Quest, page 12
10,000 years ago; almost 1,600 types of fish

Video Quest, page 17
We will be able to see life under the sea in 3D.

Apply, page 19
Answers will vary.

Analyze, page 22
Answers will vary.

Video Quest, page 25
They went into the water tank and filmed the shark and
sent the picture to a 180-degree video screen.

Choose the Correct Answers, pages 26–27
1 D **2** A **3** C **4** A **5** C **6** C **7** C **8** B

True or False?, page 27
1 T **2** T **3** F **4** T **5** F **6** T **7** F **8** T **9** T **10** F